Vegetarian Cookbook

By Don Orwell

http://SuperfoodsToday.com

D1404134

Your Free Gift

As a way of saying thanks for your purchase, I'm offering you my FREE eBook that is exclusive to my book and blog readers.

Superfoods Cookbook - Book Two has over 70 Superfoods recipes and complements Superfoods Cookbook Book One and it contains Superfoods Salads, Superfoods Smoothies and Superfoods Deserts with ultra-healthy non-refined ingredients. All ingredients are 100% Superfoods.

It also contains Superfoods Reference book which is organized by Superfoods (more than 60 of them, with the list of their benefits), Superfoods spices, all vitamins, minerals and antioxidants. Superfoods Reference Book lists Superfoods that can help with 12 diseases and 9 types of cancer.

http://www.SuperfoodsToday.com/FREE

Table of Contents

Superfoods Vegetarian Cookbook

Allergy labels: SF – Soy Free, GF – Gluten Free, DF – Dairy Free, EF – Egg Free, V - Vegan, NF – Nut Free

Condiments

Basil Pesto

- 1 cup basil
- 1/3 cup cashews
- 2 garlic cloves, chopped
- 1/2 cup olive oil

Process basil, cashews and garlic until smooth. Add oil in a slow stream. Process to combine. Transfer to a bowl. Season with salt and pepper. Stir to combine. Allergies: SF, GF, DF, EF, V

Cilantro Pesto

- 1 cup cilantro
- 1/3 cup cashews
- 2 garlic cloves, chopped
- 1/2 cup olive oil or avocado oil

Process cilantro, cashews and garlic. Add oil in a slow stream. Process to combine. Transfer to a bowl. Season with salt and pepper. Stir to combine. Allergies: SF, GF, DF, EF, V

Sundried Tomato Pesto

- 3/4 cup sundried tomatoes
- 1/3 cup cashews
- 2 garlic cloves, chopped
- 1/2 cup olive oil or avocado oil

Process tomato, cashews and garlic. Add oil in a slow stream. Process to combine. Transfer to a bowl. Season with salt and pepper. Stir to combine. Allergies: SF, GF, DF, EF, V

Broths

Some recipes require a cup or more of vegetable broth. I usually cook the whole pot and freeze it.

Vegetable broth

Servings: 6 cups

Ingredients

- 1 tbsp. coconut oil
- 1 large onion
- 2 stalks celery, including some leaves
- 2 large carrots
- 1 bunch green onions, chopped
- 8 cloves garlic, minced
- 8 sprigs fresh parsley
- 6 sprigs fresh thyme
- 2 bay leaves
- 1 tsp. salt
- 2 quarts water

Instructions - Allergies: SF, GF, DF, EF, V, NF

Chop veggies into small chunks. Heat oil in a soup pot and add onion, scallions, celery, carrots, garlic, parsley, thyme, and bay leaves. Cook over high heat for 5 to 7 minutes, stirring occasionally.

Bring to a boil and add salt. Lower heat and simmer, uncovered, for 30 minutes. Strain. Other ingredients to consider: broccoli stalk, celery root

Pastes

Curry Paste

This should not be prepared in advance, but there are several curry recipes that are using curry paste and I decided to take the curry paste recipe out and have it separately. So, when you see that the recipe is using curry paste, please go to this part of the book and prepare it from scratch. Don't use processed curry pastes or curry powder; make it every time from scratch. Keep the spices in original form (seeds, pods), ground them just before making the curry paste. You can dry heat in the skillet cloves, cardamom, cumin and coriander and then crush them coarsely with mortar and pestle.

Ingredients

- 2 onions, minced
- 2 cloves garlic, minced
- 2 teaspoons fresh ginger root, finely chopped
- 6 whole cloves

- 2 cardamom pods
- 2 (2 inch) pieces cinnamon sticks, crushed
- 1 tsp. ground cumin
- 1 tsp. ground coriander
- 1 tsp. salt
- 1 tsp. ground cayenne pepper
- 1 tsp. ground turmeric

Instructions - Allergies: SF, GF, DF, EF, V, NF

Heat oil in a frying pan over medium heat and fry onions until transparent. Stir in garlic, cumin, ginger, cloves, cinnamon, coriander, salt, cayenne, and turmeric. Cook for 1 minute over medium heat, stirring constantly. At this point other curry ingredients should be added.

Tomato paste

Some recipes (chili) require tomato paste. I usually prepare 20 or so liters at once (when tomato is in season, which is usually September) and freeze it.

Ingredients

- 5 lbs. chopped plum tomatoes
- 1/4 cup extra-virgin olive oil or avocado oil plus 2 tbsp.
- salt, to taste

Instructions - Allergies: SF, GF, DF, EF, V, NF

Heat 1/4 cup of the oil in a skillet over medium heat. Add tomatoes. Season with salt. Bring to a boil. Cook, stirring, until very soft, about 8 minutes.

Pass the tomatoes through the finest plate of a food mill. Push as much of the pulp through the sieve as possible and leave the seeds behind.

Bring it to boil, lower it and then boil uncovered, so the liquid will thicken (approx. 30-40 minutes). That will give you homemade tomato juice. You get tomato paste if you boil for 60 minutes, it gets thick like store bought ketchup.

Store sealed in an airtight container in the refrigerator for up to one month, or freeze, for up to 6 months.

Precooked beans

Again, some recipes require that you cook some beans (butter beans, red kidney, garbanzo) in advance. Cooking beans takes around 3 hours and it can be done in advance or every few weeks and the rest get frozen. Soak beans for 24 hours before cooking them. After the first boil, throw the water, add new water and continue cooking. Some beans or lentils can be sprouted for few days before cooking and that helps people with stomach problems.

Breakfast - Oatmeal

Superfoods Oatmeal Breakfast

Serves 1 - Allergies: SF, GF, DF, EF, V, NF

- 1 cup cooked oatmeal

- 1 tsp. of ground flax seeds

- 1 tsp. of sunflower seeds

- A dash of cinnamon

- Half of the tsp. of cocoa

Cook oatmeal with hot water and after that mix all ingredients. Sweeten if you have to with few drops of raw honey. Optional: You can replace sunflower seeds with pumpkin seed or chia seed. You can add a handful of blueberries or any berries instead of cocoa.

Nutrition Facts

Serving Size 52 g

Amount Per Serving

Calories 207   Calories from Fat 58

                                  % Daily Value*

Total Fat 6.4g	**10%**
Saturated Fat 0.9g	**4%**
Cholesterol 0mg	**0%**
Sodium 5mg	**0%**
Potassium 246mg	**7%**
Total Carbohydrates 28.8g	**10%**
Dietary Fiber 7.3g	**29%**
Sugars 0.5g	
Protein 8.2g	

Vitamin A 0%   •   Vitamin C 0%

Calcium 4%   •   Iron 13%

Nutrition Grade A-

* Based on a 2000 calorie diet

Oatmeal Yogurt Breakfast

Serves 1 - Allergies: SF, GF, EF, NF

• 1/2 cup dry oatmeal

• Handful of blueberries (optional)

• 1 cup of low-fat yogurt

Mix all ingredients and wait 20 minutes or leave overnight in the fridge if using steel cut oats.

Nutrition Facts

Serving Size 247 g

Amount Per Serving

Calories 255	Calories from Fat 37
	% Daily Value*
Total Fat 4.2g	6%
Saturated Fat 2.1g	11%
Cholesterol 11mg	4%
Sodium 131mg	5%
Potassium 557mg	16%
Total Carbohydrates 36.6g	12%
Dietary Fiber 3.6g	15%
Sugars 16.8g	
Protein 14.3g	

Vitamin A 2%	•	Vitamin C 12%
Calcium 35%	•	Iron 10%

Nutrition Grade A

* Based on a 2000 calorie diet

Cocoa Oatmeal

Serves 1

Ingredients - Allergies: SF, GF, DF, NF

- 1/2 cup oats
- 2 cups water
- A pinch tsp. salt
- 1/2 tsp. ground vanilla bean
- 2 tbsp. cocoa powder
- 1 tbsp. raw honey
- 2 tbsp. ground flax seeds meal
- a dash of cinnamon
- 2 egg whites

Instructions

In a saucepan over high heat, place the oats and salt. Cover with 3 cups water. Bring to a boil and cook for 3-5 minutes, stirring occasionally. Keep adding 1/2 cup water if necessary as the mixture thickens.

In a separate bowl, whisk 4 tbsp. water into the 4 tbsp. cocoa powder to form a smooth sauce. Add the vanilla to the pan and stir.

Turn the heat down to low. Add the egg whites and whisk immediately. Add the flax meal, and cinnamon. Stir to combine. Remove from heat, add raw honey and serve immediately.

Topping suggestions: sliced strawberries, blueberries or few almonds.

Flax and Blueberry Vanilla Overnight Oats

Serves 1

Ingredients - Allergies: SF, GF, EF, V, NF

- 1/2 cup oats
- 1/3 cup water
- 1/4 cup low-fat yogurt
- 1/2 tsp. ground vanilla bean
- 1 tbsp. flax seeds meal
- A pinch of salt
- Blueberries, almonds, blackberries, raw honey for topping

Instructions

Add the ingredients (except for toppings) to the bowl in the evening. Refrigerate overnight.

In the morning, stir up the mixture. It should be thick. Add the toppings of your choice.

Apple Oatmeal

Serves 1

Ingredients - Allergies: SF, GF, DF, EF, V, NF

- 1 grated apple
- 1/2 cup oats
- 1 cup water
- Dash of cinnamon
- 2 tsp. raw honey

Instructions

Cook the oats with the water for 3-5 minutes.

Add grated apple and cinnamon. Stir in the raw honey.

Almond Butter Banana Oats

Serves 1

Ingredients - Allergies: SF, GF

- 1/2 cup oats
- 3/4 cup water
- 1 egg white
- 1 banana
- 1 tbs. flax seeds meal
- 1 tsp raw honey
- pinch cinnamon
- 1/2 tbs. almond butter

Instructions

Combine oats and water in a bowl. Beat the egg white, then whisk it in with the uncooked oats. Boil on stovetop. Check consistency and continue to heat as necessary until the oats are fluffy and thick. Mash banana and add to oats. Heat for 1 minute

Stir in flax, raw honey, and cinnamon. Top with almond butter!

Coconut Pomegranate Oatmeal

Serves 1

Ingredients - Allergies: SF, GF, DF, EF, V, NF

- 1/2 cup oats
- 1/3 cup coconut milk
- 1 cup water
- 2 tbs. shredded unsweetened coconut
- 1-2 tbs. flax seeds meal
- 1 tbs. raw honey
- 3 tbs. pomegranate seeds

Instructions

Cook oats with the coconut milk, water, and salt.

Stir in the coconut, raw honey and flaxseed meal. Sprinkle with extra coconut and pomegranate seeds.

Savory Breakfasts

Serves 1

Regular egg recipes

Allergies: SF, GF, DF, NF

Eggs are great way to start a day and you can enjoy them hard boiled, scrambled, poached or in the omelet with veggies. Eat some breakfast veggies with eggs.

Omelet with Leeks

Serves 1 - Allergies: SF, GF, DF, NF

Cook leeks in little coconut oil until they get soft and then mix the beaten eggs in.

Egg pizza crust

Ingredients - Allergies: SF, GF, DF, NF

- 3 eggs
- 1/2 cup of coconut flour
- 1 cup of coconut milk
- 1 crushed garlic clove

Mix and make an omelet.

Omelet with Superfoods veggies

Serves 1

Ingredients - Allergies: SF, GF, DF, NF

- 2 large eggs

- Salt

- Ground black pepper

- 1 tsp. olive oil or cumin oil

- 1 cup spinach, cherry tomatoes and 1 spoon of yogurt cheese

- Crushed red pepper flakes and a pinch of dill (optional)

Instructions

Whisk 2 large eggs in a small bowl. Season with salt and ground black pepper and set aside. Heat 1 tsp. olive oil in a medium skillet over medium heat. Add baby spinach, tomatoes, cheese and cook, tossing, until wilted (Approx. 1 minute). Add eggs; cook, stirring occasionally, until just set, about 1 minute. Stir in cheese. Sprinkle with crushed red pepper flakes and dill.

Egg Muffins

Ingredients - Allergies: SF, GF, DF, NF

Serving: 8 muffins

- 8 eggs

- 1 cup diced green bell pepper

- 1 cup diced onion

- 1 cup spinach

- 1/4 tsp. salt

- 1/8 tsp. ground black pepper

- 2 tbsp. water

Instructions

Heat the oven to 350 degrees F. Oil 8 muffin cups. Beat eggs together. Mix in bell pepper, spinach, onion, salt, black pepper, and water. Pour the mixture into muffin cups. Bake in the oven until muffins are done in the middle.

Egg Bake

Ingredients - Allergies: SF, GF, DF, NF

Serves 6

- 2 cups chopped red peppers or spinach
- 1 cup zucchini
- 2 tbsp. coconut oil
- 1 cup sliced mushrooms
- 1/2 cup sliced green onions
- 8 eggs
- 1 cup coconut milk
- 1/2 cup almond flour
- 2 tbsp. minced fresh parsley
- 1/2 tsp. dried basil
- 1/2 tsp. salt
- 1/4 tsp. ground black pepper

Instructions

Preheat oven to 350 degrees F. Put coconut oil in a skillet. Heat it to medium heat. Add mushrooms, onions, zucchini and red pepper (or spinach) until vegetables are tender, about 5 minutes. Drain veggies and spread them over the baking dish.

Beat eggs in a bowl with milk, flour, parsley, basil, salt, and pepper. Pour egg mixture into baking dish.

Bake in preheated oven until the center is set (approx. 35 to 40 minutes).

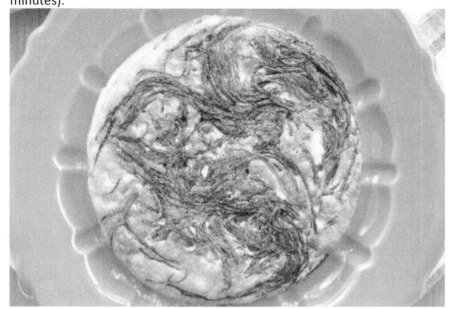

Frittata

6 servings

Ingredients - Allergies: SF, GF, DF, NF

- 2 tbsp. olive oil or avocado oil
- 1 Zucchini, sliced
- 1 cup torn fresh spinach
- 2 tbsp. sliced green onions
- 1 tsp. crushed garlic, salt and pepper to taste
- 1/3 cup coconut milk
- 6 eggs

Instructions

Heat olive oil in a skillet over medium heat. Add zucchini and cook until tender. Mix in spinach, green onions, and garlic. Season with salt and pepper. Continue cooking until spinach is wilted.

In a separate bowl, beat together eggs and coconut milk. Pour into the skillet over the vegetables. Reduce heat to low, cover, and cook until eggs are firm (5 to 7 minutes).

Superfoods Naan / Pancakes / Crepes

Ingredients - Allergies: SF, GF, DF, EF, V

- 1/2 cup almond flour
- 1/2 cup Tapioca Flour
- 1 cup Coconut Milk
- Salt
- coconut oil

Instructions

Mix all the ingredients together.

Heat a pan over medium heat and pour batter to desired thickness. Once the batter looks firm, flip it over to cook the other side.

If you want this to be a dessert crepe or pancake, then omit the salt. You can add minced garlic or ginger in the batter if you want, or some spices.

Zucchini Pancakes

Serves 3

Ingredients - Allergies: SF, GF, DF

- 2 medium zucchini
- 2 tbsp. chopped onion
- 3 beaten eggs
- 6 to 8 tbsp. almond flour
- 1 tsp. salt
- 1/2 tsp. ground black pepper
- coconut oil

Instructions

Heat the oven to 300 degrees F.

Grate the zucchini into a bowl and stir in the onion and eggs. Stir in 6 tbsp. of the flour, salt, and pepper.

Heat a large sauté pan over medium heat and add coconut oil in the pan. When the oil is hot, lower the heat to medium-low and add batter into the pan. Cook the pancakes about 2 minutes on each side, until browned. Place the pancakes in the oven.

Savory Superfoods Pie Crust

Ingredients - Allergies: SF, GF, DF

- 11/4 cups blanched almond flour
- 1/3 cup tapioca flour
- 3/4 tsp. finely ground sea salt
- 3/4 tsp. paprika
- 1/2 tsp. ground cumin
- 1/8 tsp. ground white pepper
- 1/4 cup coconut oil
- 1 large egg

Instructions

Instructions

Place almond flour, tapioca flour, sea salt, vanilla, egg and coconut sugar (if you use coconut sugar) in the bowl of a food processor. Process 2-3 times to combine. Add oil and raw honey (if you use raw honey) and pulse with several one-second pulses and then let the food processor run until the mixture comes together. Move dough onto a plastic wrap sheet. Wrap and then press the dough into a 9-inch disk. Refrigerate for 30 minutes.

Remove plastic wrap. Press dough onto the bottom and up the sides of a 9-inch buttered pie dish. Crimp a little bit the edges of crust. Cool in the refrigerator for 20 minutes. Put the oven rack to middle position and preheat oven to 375F. Put in the oven and bake until golden brown.

Quiche

Serves 2-3

Ingredients - Allergies: SF, GF, DF, NF

- 1 Precooked and cooled Savory Superfoods Pie Crust
- 8 ounces organic spinach, cooked and drained
- 2 medium shallots, thinly sliced and sautéed
- 4 large eggs
- 1 cup coconut milk
- 3/4 tsp. salt
- 1/4 tsp. freshly ground black pepper

Instructions

Heat coconut oil and add spinach and shallots. Set aside once done.

Preheat oven to 350F. In a large bowl, combine eggs, milk, salt and pepper. Whisk until foamy. Add in about 3/4 of the drained filling mixture, reserving the other 1/4 to "top" the quiche. Pour egg mixture into crust and place remaining filling on top of the quiche.

Place quiche in oven in the center of the middle rack and bake undisturbed for 45 to 50 minutes.

Cottage Cheese Sesame Balls

Ingredients - Allergies: SF, GF, EF

- 16 ounce farmers cheese or cottage cheese
- 1 cup finely chopped almonds
- 1and 1/2 cups oatmeal

In a large bowl, combine blended cottage cheese, almonds and oatmeal. Make balls and roll in sesame seeds mix.

Superfoods Smoothies

Put the liquid in first. Surrounded by tea or yogurt, the blender blades can move freely. Next, add chunks of fruits or vegetables. Leafy greens are going into the pitcher last. Preferred liquid is green tea, but you can use almond or coconut milk or herbal tea.

Start slow. If your blender has speeds, start it on low to break up big pieces of fruit. Continue blending until you get a puree. If your blender can pulse, pulse a few times before switching to a puree mode. Once you have your liquid and fruit pureed, start adding greens, very slowly. Wait until previous batch of greens has been completely blended.

Thicken? Added too much tea or coconut milk? Thicken your smoothie by adding ice cubes, flax meal, chia seeds or oatmeal. Once you get used to various tastes of smoothies, add any seaweed, spirulina, chlorella powder or ginger for additional kick. Experiment with any Superfoods in powder form at this point. Think of adding any nut butter or sesame paste too or some Superfoods oils.

Rotate! Rotate your greens; don't always drink the same smoothie! At the beginning try 2 different greens every week and later introduce third and fourth one weekly. And keep rotating them. Don't use spinach and kale all the time. Try beets greens, they have a pinch of pink in them and that add great color to your smoothie. Here is the list of leafy green for you to try: spinach, kale, dandelion, chards, beet leaves, arugula, lettuce, collard greens, bok choy, cabbage, cilantro, parsley.

Flavor! Flavor smoothies with ground vanilla bean, cinnamon, raw honey, nutmeg, cloves, almond butter, cayenne pepper, ginger or just about any seeds or chopped nuts combination.

Not only are green smoothies high in nutrients, vitamins and fiber, they can also make any vegetable you probably don't like (be it kale, spinach or broccoli) taste great. The secret behind blending the perfect smoothie is using sweet fruits or nuts or seeds to give your drink a unique taste.

There's a reason kale and spinach seem to be the main ingredients in almost every green smoothie. Not only do they give smoothies their verdant color, they are also packed with calcium, protein and iron.

Although blending alone increases the accessibility of carotenoids, since the presence of fats is known to increase carotenoid absorption from leafy greens, it is possible that coconut oil, nuts and seeds in a smoothie could increase absorption further.

If you can't find some ingredient, replace it with the closest one.

GREEN SMOOTHIES

Kale Kiwi Smoothie

- 1 cup Kale, chopped

- 2 Apples

- 3 Kiwis

- 1 tablespoon flax seeds

- 1 tablespoon royal jelly

- 1 cup crushed ice

Zucchini Apples Smoothie

- 1/2 cup zucchini

- 2 Apples

- 3/4 avocado

- 1 stalk Celery

- 1 Lemon

- 1 tbsp. Spirulina

- 1 1/2 cups crushed ice

Dandelion Smoothie

- 1 cup Dandelion greens

- 1 cup Spinach

- ½ cup tahini

- 1 Red Radish

- 1 tbsp. chia seeds

- 1 cup lavender tea

Fennel Honeydew Smoothie

- ½ cup fennel

- 1 cup Broccoli

- 1 tbsp. Cilantro

- 1 cup Honeydew

- 1 cup crushed ice

- 1 tbsp. Chlorella

Broccoli Apple Smoothie

- 1 Apple

- 1 cup Broccoli

- 1 tbsp. Cilantro

- 1 Celery stalk

- 1 cup crushed ice

- 1 tbsp. crushed Seaweed

Salad Smoothie

- 1 cup spinach
- ½ cucumber
- 1/2 small onion
- 2 tablespoons Parsley
- 2 tablespoons lemon juice
- 1 cup crushed ice
- 1 tbsp. olive oil or cumin oil
- ¼ cup Wheatgrass

Avocado Kale Smoothie

- 1 cup Kale

- ½ Avocado

- 1 cup Cucumber

- 1 Celery Stalk

- 1 tbsp. chia seeds

- 1 cup chamomile tea

- 1 tbsp. Spirulina

Watercress Smoothie

- 1 cup Watercress

- ½ cup almond butter

- 2 small cucumbers

- 1 cup coconut milk

- 1 tbsp. Chlorella

- 1 tbsp. Black cumin seeds – sprinkle on top and garnish with parsley

Beet Greens Smoothie

- 1 cup Beet Greens

- 2 tbsp. Pumpkin seeds butter

- 1 cup Strawberry

- 1 tbsp. Sesame seeds

- 1 tbsp. hemp seeds

- 1 cup chamomile tea

Broccoli Leeks Cucumber smoothie

- 1 cup Broccoli

- 2 tbsp. Cashew butter

- 2 Leeks

- 2 Cucumbers

- 1 Lime

- ½ cup Lettuce

- ½ cup Leaf Lettuce

- 1 tbsp. Matcha

- 1 cup crushed ice

Cacao Spinach Smoothie

- 2 cups spinach

- 1 cup blueberries, frozen

- 1 tablespoons dark cocoa powder

- ½ cup unsweetened almond milk

- 1/2 cup crushed ice

- 1 tsp raw honey

- 1 tbsp. Matcha powder

Flax Almond Butter Smoothie

- ½ cup plain yogurt

- 2 tablespoons almond butter

- 2 cups spinach

- 1 banana, frozen

- 3 strawberries

- 1/2 cup crushed ice

- 1 teaspoon flax seeds

Apple Kale Smoothie

- 1 cup kale

- ½ cup coconut milk

- 1 tbsp. Maca

- 1 banana, frozen

- ¼ teaspoon cinnamon

- 1 Apple

- Pinch of nutmeg

- 1 clove

- 3 ice cubes

Iceberg Peach Smoothie

- 1 cup Iceberg lettuce

- 1 Banana

- 1 peach

- 1 Brazil Nut

- 1 Mango

- 1 cup Kombucha

- Top with hemp seeds

Rainbow Smoothie

3 Colors Rainbow Smoothie

- Blend 1 Large beet with some crushed ice

- Blend 3 carrots with some crashed ice

- Blend 1 cucumber, 1 cup of leaf lettuce and ½ cup Wheatgrass

- Serve them separate to preserve the distinct color

Salad Dressings

Italian Dressing

Serves 1 - Allergies: SF, GF, DF, EF, V, NF

- 1 tsp. olive oil or cumin oil
- lemon
- minced garlic
- salt
- 1 Tbsp. of Spirulina, Chlorella, Maca or Matcha (optional)

Yogurt Dressing

Serves 1 - Allergies: SF, GF, DF, EF, V, NF

- half a cup of plain low-fat Greek yogurt or low-fat buttermilk
- olive oil or avocado oil
- minced garlic
- salt
- lemon

Occasionally I would add a tsp. of mustard or some herbs like basil, oregano, marjoram, chives, thyme, parsley, dill or mint. If you like spicy hot food, add some cayenne in the dressing. It will speed up your metabolism and have interesting hot spicy effect in cold yogurt or buttermilk.

Salads

Large Fiber Loaded Salad with Italian Dressing

Serves 1 - Allergies: SF, GF, EF, NF

- 1 cup of spinach

- 1 cup of shredded cabbage, sauerkraut or lettuce. Cabbage has more substance.

- Italian or Yogurt dressing

- Cayenne pepper (optional)

- Few sprigs of cilantro (optional)

- 2 spring (green) onions (optional)

Nutrition Facts

Serving Size 105 g

Amount Per Serving

Calories 64	Calories from Fat 44
	% Daily Value*
Total Fat 4.9g	**7%**
Saturated Fat 0.7g	**4%**
Cholesterol 0mg	**0%**
Sodium 36mg	**2%**
Potassium 286mg	**8%**
Total Carbohydrates 5.1g	**2%**
Dietary Fiber 2.4g	**10%**
Sugars 2.4g	
Protein 1.8g	

Vitamin A 58%	•	Vitamin C 57%
Calcium 6%	•	Iron 6%

Nutrition Grade A

* Based on a 2000 calorie diet

Large Fiber Loaded Salad with Yogurt Dressing

Serves 1 - Allergies: SF, GF, EF, NF

- 1 cup of spinach

- 1 cup of shredded cabbage or lettuce. Cabbage has more substance.

- Italian or Yogurt dressing

- Cayenne pepper (optional)

- Few sprigs of cilantro (optional)

- 2 spring (green) onions (optional)

Nutrition Facts

Serving Size 226 g

Amount Per Serving

Calories 136	Calories from Fat 40

	% Daily Value*
Total Fat 4.5g	**7%**
Saturated Fat 1.7g	**8%**
Cholesterol 7mg	**2%**
Sodium 122mg	**5%**
Potassium 573mg	**16%**
Total Carbohydrates 13.8g	**5%**
Dietary Fiber 2.4g	**10%**
Sugars 11.0g	
Protein 8.7g	

Vitamin A 59%	•	Vitamin C 58%
Calcium 28%	•	Iron 7%

Nutrition Grade A

* Based on a 2000 calorie diet

Large Fiber Loaded Salad as a meal on its own – only 258 calories per serving

Serves 1 - Allergies: SF, GF, EF, NF

This is what I eat every second evening and I can't get enough of it!!! This is the real secret to lose weight while having full stomach with grade A ingredients!!

- 1 cup of spinach

- 1 cup of shredded cabbage

- Yogurt dressing

- Cayenne pepper (optional)

- Few sprigs of cilantro (optional)

- 2 spring (green) onions

- 5 oz. low-fat farmers cheese

Pour yogurt dressing into the salad bowl. Add farmers' cheese and mix thoroughly. Cut spring onions in small pieces and add to the cheese mixture and mix. Add spinach and cabbage and mix thoroughly. Add spices (optional).

Nutrition Facts

Serving Size 401 g

Amount Per Serving

Calories 258   Calories from Fat 62

	% Daily Value*
Total Fat 6.8g	**11%**
Saturated Fat 2.0g	**10%**
Cholesterol 7mg	**2%**
Sodium 708mg	**30%**
Potassium 656mg	**19%**
Total Carbohydrates 21.5g	**7%**
Dietary Fiber 3.2g	**13%**
Sugars 15.9g	
Protein 26.6g	

Vitamin A 65%	•	Vitamin C 68%
Calcium 30%	•	Iron 9%

Nutrition Grade A-

* Based on a 2000 calorie diet

Greek Salad

Serves 4 - Allergies: SF, GF, EF, NF

- 1 head iceberg lettuce
- 1 head romaine lettuce
- 1 lb. plump tomatoes
- 6 oz. Greek or black olives, sliced
- 4 oz. sliced radishes
- 4 oz. low-fat feta or goat cheese

Dressing:
- 3 oz. olive oil or avocado oil
- 3 oz. fresh lemon juice
- 1 tsp. dried oregano
- 1 tsp. black pepper
- 1 tsp. salt
- 4 cloves garlic, minced

Wash and cut lettuce into pieces. Slice tomatoes in quarters. Combine olives, lettuce, tomatoes, and radishes in large bowl. Mix dressing ingredients together and toss with vegetables. Pour out into a shallow serving bowl. Crumble feta/goat cheese over on top.

Cucumber, Cilantro, Quinoa Tabbouleh

Serves 2

Ingredients - Allergies: SF, GF, DF, EF, NF, V

- 1 cup cooked quinoa mixed with 1 tbsp. sesame seeds
- 1/2 cup chopped tomato and green pepper
- 1 cup chopped cucumber
- 1/2 cup chopped cilantro

Dressing:
- 1 tbsp. olive oil or cumin oil
- 1 tbsp. fresh lemon juice
- pinch of black pepper
- pinch of sea salt

Instructions: Mix all ingredients.

Almond, Quinoa, Red Peppers & Arugula Salad

Serves 2

Ingredients - Allergies: SF, GF, DF, EF, NF, V

- 1 cup cooked quinoa mixed with 1 tbsp. pumpkin seeds
- 1/2 cup chopped almonds
- 1 cup chopped arugula
- 1/2 cup sliced red peppers

Dressing:
- 1 tbsp. olive oil or cumin oil
- 1 tbsp. fresh lemon juice
- pinch of black pepper
- pinch of sea salt

Instructions: Mix all ingredients.

Asparagus, Quinoa & Red Peppers Salad

Serves 2

Ingredients - Allergies: SF, GF, DF, EF, NF, V

- 1 cup cooked quinoa mixed with 1 tbsp. sunflower seeds
- 1 cup sliced red peppers
- 1 cup grilled asparagus
- Garnish with lime and parsley

Dressing:
- 1 tbsp. olive oil or avocado oil
- 1 tbsp. fresh lemon juice
- pinch of black pepper
- pinch of sea salt

Instructions: Mix all ingredients.

Chickpeas, Quinoa, Cucumber & Tomato Salad

Serves 2

Ingredients - Allergies: SF, GF, DF, EF, NF, V

- 1 cup cooked <u>quinoa</u> mixed with 1 tbsp. sesame seeds
- 1 cup cooked chickpeas
- 1 cup chopped cucumber and green onions
- 1/2 cup chopped tomato

Dressing:
- 1 tbsp. <u>olive</u> oil or <u>avocado</u> oil
- 1 tbsp. fresh lemon juice
- pinch of black pepper
- pinch of sea salt

Instructions: Mix all ingredients.

Strawberry Spinach Salad
Serves 4-6

Ingredients - Allergies: SF, GF, DF, EF, V

- 2 tbsp. black sesame seeds
- 1 tbsp. poppy seeds
- 1/2 cup olive oil or avocado oil
- 1/4 cup lemon juice
- 1/4 tsp. paprika
- 1 bag fresh spinach - chopped, washed and dried
- 1 quart strawberries, sliced
- 1/4 cup toasted slivered almonds

Instructions

Whisk together the sesame seeds, olive oil, poppy seeds, paprika, lemon juice and onion. Refrigerate.
In a large bowl, combine the spinach, strawberries and almonds. Pour dressing over salad. Toss and refrigerate 15 minutes before serving.

Cauliflower & Eggs Salad

Serves 1

Ingredients - Allergies: SF, GF, NF

- 1 cup chopped Cauliflower
- 2 hardboiled eggs - chopped,
- 2 oz. shredded cheddar cheese, low-fat
- 1 red onion, celery,
- 1 dill pickles,
- 1 tbsp. yellow mustard.

Mix all ingredients.

Quinoa & almond Superfoods Tabbouleh
Serves 2-3

Ingredients - Allergies: SF, GF, EF

- 2 cups cooked quinoa
- 1 bunch mint, leaves picked & 1 bunch flat leaf parsley
- 1/2 small red onion, finely chopped
- 1/4 Cup lemon juice& 1/4 Cup extra virgin olive oil or avocado oil
- 1/2 Cup whole almonds & 1/2 cup chia or sunflower seeds
- 1 Cup cherry tomatoes & 1 Avocado optional
- 1 Cup chopped Kale or Dandelion
- Low fat yogurt, to serve, optional

Instructions

Cook quinoa and let it cool. Chop off and discard half of the parsley stalks. Finely chop the remaining parsley bunch, mint and greens. Stir herbs in a salad bowl and add onion to drained quinoa. Combine lemon juice and olive oil and season well. Add other ingredients, mix and dress salad.

Greek Cucumber Salad

Serves 2-3

Ingredients - Allergies: SF, GF, EF, NF

- 2-3 cucumbers, sliced
- 2 teaspoons salt
- 3 tbsp. lemon juice
- 1/4 tsp. paprika
- 1/4 tsp. white pepper
- 1/2 clove garlic, minced
- 4 fresh green onions, diced
- 1 cup thick Greek Yogurt

- 1/4 tsp. paprika

Instructions

Slice cucumbers thinly, sprinkle with salt and mix. Set aside for one hour. Mix lemon juice, water, garlic, paprika and white pepper, and set aside. Squeeze liquid from cucumber slices a few at a time, and place slices in the bowl. Discard liquid. Add lemon juice mixture, green onions, and yogurt. Mix and sprinkle additional paprika or dill over top. Chill for 1-2 hours.

Mediterranean Salad

Serves 3-4

Ingredients - Allergies: SF, GF, DF, EF, V, NF

- 1 medium head romaine lettuce, torn
- 3 small tomatoes, diced
- 1 medium cucumber, sliced
- 1 small green bell pepper, sliced
- 1 small onion, cut into rings
- 6 radishes, thinly sliced
- 1/2 cup flat leaf parsley, chopped
- 1/3 cup olive oil or avocado oil
- 3 tbsp. lemon juice
- 1 garlic clove, minced
- Salt & pepper
- 1 tsp. fresh mint, minced

Instructions

Combine lettuce, tomatoes, cucumber, pepper, onion, radishes & parsley in a salad bowl. Whisk together olive oil, lemon juice, garlic, salt, pepper & mint. Pour over salad & toss to coat.

Pomegranate Avocado salad

Serves 1

Ingredients - Allergies: SF, GF, DF, EF, V

- 1 cup mixed greens, spinach, arugula, red leaf lettuce
- 1 ripe avocado, cut into 1/2-inch pieces
- 1/2 cup pomegranate seeds
- 1/4 cup pecan
- 1/4 cup blackberries
- 1/4 cup cherry tomatoes
- olive oil or avocado oil, salt, lemon juice

Instructions

Combine greens, pecan, cut avocado, tomatoes, pomegranates and blackberries in a salad bowl. Whisk together salt, olive oil and lemon juice and pour over salad.

Superfoods Salad

Allergies: SF, GF

Typical superfoods salad should have:

1 part leafy greens - kale, spinach, dandelion and optional cilantro

1 part veggies -carrots, tomato, peppers, beets, broccoli, celery, and some pungent veggies - shallots, ginger or garlic

1 part fruits - pomegranates, avocado, blackberries, blueberries, sliced apple, grapefruit, raspberries, orange

1/2 part of nuts & seeds - almond, walnuts, chia, flax meal, sunflower seeds, pumpkin seeds

1 part protein - low-fat feta, yogurt or 2 boiled eggs

1 part cooked quinoa (optional)

Make your own mix and use different ingredient every time

Roasted Beet Salad

Serves 3-4

Instructions - Allergies: SF, GF, DF, EF, V, NF

Toss 4 beets cut in half in a baking dish with olive oil, salt and pepper. Cover and roast at 425 degrees F until tender; let cool, then rub off the skins. Toss with any juices from the baking dish, capers, chopped pickles, a dash each of hot sauce, and chopped parsley or dill.

Apple Coleslaw

Serves 1-2

Ingredients - Allergies: SF, GF, DF, EF, V, NF

- 1 cup chopped cabbage (various color)
- 1 tart apple chopped
- 1 celery, chopped
- 1 red pepper chopped
- 5 tsp. olive oil or avocado oil
- juice of 1 lemon
- 2 Tbs raw honey (optional)
- dash sea salt

Instructions

Toss the cabbage, apple, celery, and pepper together in a large bowl. In a smaller bowl, whisk remaining ingredients. Drizzle over coleslaw and toss to coat.

Appetizers

Deviled Eggs

Allergies: SF, GF, DF, NF

Make deviled eggs and optionally add some chopped green chilies, black olives, chili powder and cayenne.

Hummus

Ingredients - Allergies: SF, GF, DF, EF, V, NF

- 2 cups cooked chickpeas (garbanzo beans)
- 1/4 cup (59 ml) fresh lemon juice, about 1 large lemon
- 1/4 cup (59 ml) tahini
- Half of a large garlic clove, minced
- 2 tbsp. olive oil or cumin oil, plus more for serving
- 1/2 to 1 tsp. salt
- 1/2 tsp. ground cumin
- 2 to 3 tbsp. water
- Dash of ground paprika for serving

Instructions

Combine tahini and lemon juice and blend for 1 minute. Add the olive oil, minced garlic, cumin and the salt to tahini and lemon mixture. Process for 30 seconds, scrape sides and then process 30 seconds more.

Add half of the chickpeas to the food processor and process for 1 minute. Scrape sides, add remaining chickpeas and process for 1 to 2 minutes.

Transfer the hummus into a bowl then drizzle about 1 tbsp. of olive oil over the top and sprinkle with paprika.

Guacamole

Ingredients - Allergies: SF, GF, DF, EF, V, NF

- 4 ripe avocados
- 3 tbsp. freshly squeezed lemon juice (1 lemon)
- 8 dashes hot pepper sauce
- 1/2 cup diced onion
- 1 large garlic clove, minced
- 1 tsp. salt
- 1 tsp. ground black pepper
- 1 medium tomato, seeded, and small-diced

Instructions

Cut the avocados in half, remove the pits, and scoop the flesh out. Immediately add the lemon juice, hot pepper sauce, garlic, onion, salt, and pepper and toss well. Dice avocados. Add the tomatoes. Mix well and taste for salt and pepper.

Baba Ghanoush

Ingredients - Allergies: SF, GF, DF, EF, V, NF

- 1 large eggplant
- 1/4 cup tahini, plus more as needed
- 3 garlic cloves, minced
- 1/4 cup fresh lemon juice, plus more as needed
- 1 pinch ground cumin
- salt, to taste
- 1 tbsp. extra-virgin olive oil or avocado oil
- 1 tbsp. chopped flat-leaf parsley
- 1/4 cup brine-cured black olives, such as Kalamata

Instructions:

Grill eggplant for 10 to 15 minutes. Heat the oven (375 F).

Put the eggplant to a baking sheet and bake 15-20 minutes or until very soft. Remove from the oven, let cool, and peel off and discard the skin. Put the eggplant flesh in a bowl. Using a fork, mash the eggplant to a paste.

Add the 1/4 cup tahini, garlic, cumin, 1/4 cup lemon juice and mix well. Season with salt to taste. Transfer the mixture to a serving bowl and spread with the back of a spoon to form a shallow well. Drizzle the olive oil over the top and sprinkle with the parsley.

Serve at room temperature.

Espinacase la Catalana

Serves 4

Ingredients - Allergies: SF, GF, DF, EF, V

- 2 cups spinach
- 2 cloves garlic
- 3 tbsp cashews
- 3 tbsp dried currants
- <u>olive</u> oil or <u>avocado</u> oil

Instructions

Wash the spinach and trim off the stems. Steam the spinach for few minutes.

Peel and slice the garlic. Pour a few tablespoons of olive oil and cover the bottom of a frying pan. Heat pan on medium and sauté garlic for 1-2 minutes. Add the cashews and the currants to the pan and continue to sauté for 1 minute. Add the spinach and mix well, coating with oil. Salt to taste.

Tapenade

Ingredients - Allergies: SF, GF, DF, EF, V, NF

- 1/2 pound pitted mixed olives

- 1 small clove garlic, minced

- 2 tbsp. capers

- 2 to 3 fresh basil leaves

- 1 tbsp. freshly squeezed lemon juice

- 2 tbsp. extra-virgin <u>olive</u> oil or <u>cumin</u> oil

Instructions

Rinse the olives in cool water. Place all ingredients in the bowl of a food processor. Process to combine, until it becomes a coarse paste. Transfer to a bowl and serve

Red Pepper Dip

Ingredients - Allergies: SF, GF, EF, NF

- 1 pound red peppers

- 1 cup farmers' cheese

- 1/4 cup virgin olive oil or avocado oil

- 1 tbsp minced garlic

- Lemon juice, salt, basil, oregano, red pepper flakes to taste.

Instructions

Roast the peppers. Cover them and cool for about 15 minutes. Peel the peppers and remove the seeds and stems. Chop the peppers.

Transfer the peppers and garlic to a food processor and process until smooth. Add the farmers' cheese and garlic and process until smooth. With the machine running, add olive oil and lemon juice. Add the basil, oregano, red pepper flakes, and 1/4 tsp. salt, and process until smooth. Adjust the seasoning, to taste. Pour to a bowl and refrigerate.

Roasted Garlic

Instructions - Allergies: SF, GF, DF, EF, V, NF

Heat the oven to 350 F.
Rub olive oil into the top of each garlic head and place it cut side down on a foil-lined baking sheet. Bake until the cloves turn golden. Remove from the oven and let cool. Squeeze each head of garlic to expel the cloves into a bowl. Mash into a paste.

Eggplant and Yogurt

Instructions - Allergies: SF, GF, EF, NF

Mix 1 pound chopped eggplant, 3 unpeeled shallots and 3 unpeeled garlic cloves with 1/4 cup olive oil, salt and pepper on a baking sheet. Roast at 400 degrees for half an hour. Cool and squeeze the shallots and garlic from their skins and chop. Mix with the eggplant, almond, 1/2 cup plain yogurt, dill and salt and pepper.

Caponata

Serves 3-4

Ingredients - Allergies: SF, GF, DF

- coconut oil
- 2 large eggplants, cut into large chunks
- 1 tsp. dried oregano
- Sea salt
- Freshly ground black pepper
- 1 small onion, peeled and finely chopped
- 2 cloves garlic, peeled and finely sliced
- 1 small bunch fresh flat-leaf parsley, leaves picked and stalks finely chopped
- 2 tbsp. salted capers, rinsed, soaked and drained
- 1 handful green olives, stones removed
- 2-3 tbsp. lemon juice
- 5 large ripe tomatoes, roughly chopped
- coconut oil
- 2 tbsp. slivered almonds, lightly toasted, optional

Instructions

Heat coconut oil in a pan and add eggplant, oregano and salt. Cook on a high heat for around 4 or 5 minutes. Add the onion, garlic and parsley stalks and continue cooking for another few minutes. Add drained capers and the olives and lemon juice. When all the juice has evaporated, add the tomatoes and simmer until tender.

Season with salt and olive oil to taste before serving. Sprinkle with almonds.

Soups

Cream of Broccoli Soup

Serves 4

Ingredients - Allergies: SF, GF, EF, NF

- 1 1/2 pounds broccoli, fresh
- 2 cups water
- 3/4 tsp. salt, pepper to taste
- 1/2 cup tapioca flour, mixed with 1 cup cold water
- 1/2 cup coconut cream

- 1/2 cup low-fat farmers cheese

Steam or boil broccoli until it gets tender.
Put 2 cups water and coconut cream in top of double boiler.
Add salt, cheese and pepper. Heat until cheese gets melted.
Add broccoli. Mix water and tapioca flour in a small bowl.
Stir tapioca mixture into cheese mixture in double boiler and heat until soup thickens.

Lentil Soup
Serves 4-6

Ingredients - Allergies: SF, GF, DF, EF, NF
- 2 tbsp. olive oil or avocado oil
- 1 cup finely chopped onion
- 1/2 cup chopped carrot
- 1/2 cup chopped celery
- 2 teaspoons salt
- 1 pound lentils
- 1 cup chopped tomatoes
- 2 quarts vegetable broth
- 1/2 tsp. ground coriander & toasted cumin

Instructions

Place the olive oil into a large Dutch oven. Set over medium heat. Once hot, add the celery, onion, carrot and salt and do until the onions are translucent. Add the lentils, tomatoes, cumin, broth and coriander and stir to combine. Increase the heat and bring just to a boil. Reduce the heat, cover and simmer at a low until the lentils are tender (approx. 35 to 40 minutes). Puree with a bender to your preferred consistency (optional). Serve immediately.

Cold Cucumber Avocado Soup
Serves 2-3

Ingredients - Allergies: SF, GF, EF, NF
- 1 cucumber peeled, seeded and cut into 2-inch chunks
- 1 avocado, peeled
- 2 chopped scallions
- 1 cup vegetable broth
- 3/4 cup Greek low-fat yogurt
- 2 tbsp. lemon juice
- 1/2 tsp. ground pepper, or to taste

Garnish:
- Chopped chives, dill, mint, scallions or cucumber

Instructions

Combine the cucumber, avocado and scallions in a blender. Pulse until chopped.

Add yogurt, broth and lemon juice and continue until smooth.

Season with pepper and salt to taste and chill for 4 hours.

Taste for seasoning and garnish.

Gaspacho

Serves 4

Ingredients - Allergies: SF, GF, DF, EF, V, NF

- 1/2 cup of <u>flax</u> seeds meal
- 1kg tomatoes, diced
- 1 red pepper and 1 green pepper, diced
- 1 cucumber, peeled and diced
- 2 cloves of garlic, peeled and crushed
- 150ml extra virgin <u>olive</u> oil or <u>avocado</u> oil
- 2tbsp lemon juice
- Salt, to taste

Instructions

Mix the peppers, tomatoes and cucumber with the crushed garlic and olive oil in the bowl of a blender. Add flax meal to the mixture. Blend until smooth. Add salt and lemon juice to taste and stir well. Refrigerate until well chilled. Serve with black olives, hard-boiled egg, cilantro, mint or parsley.

Creamy roasted mushroom

Serves 4

Ingredients - Allergies: SF, GF, DF, EF, V, NF

- 1 pound Portobello mushrooms, cut into 1inch pieces

- 1/2 pound shiitake mushrooms, stemmed

- 6 tbsp. <u>olive</u> oil or <u>avocado</u> oil

- 2 cups vegetable broth

- 1 1/2 tbsp. <u>coconut</u> oil

- 1 onion, chopped

- 3 garlic cloves, minced

- 3 tbsp. arrowroot flour

- 1 cup coconut cream

- 3/4 tsp. chopped thyme

Instructions

Heat oven to 400°F. Line one large baking sheets with foil. Spread mushrooms and drizzle some olive oil on them. Season with salt and pepper and toss. Cover with foil and bake them for half an hour. Uncover and continue baking 15 minutes more. Cool slightly. Mix one half of the mushrooms with one can of broth in a blender. Set aside.

Melt coconut oil in a large pot over high heat. Add onion and garlic and sauté until onion is translucent. Add flour and stir 2 minutes. Add cream, broth, and thyme. Stir in remaining cooked mushrooms and mushroom puree. Simmer over low heat until thickened (approx. 10 minutes). Season to taste with salt and pepper.

Black Bean Soup
Serves 6-8

Ingredients - Allergies: SF, GF, DF, EF, NF

- 1/4 cup coconut oil
- 1/4 cup Onion, Diced
- 1/4 cup Carrots, Diced
- 1/4 cup Green Bell Pepper, Diced
- 1 cup vegetable broth
- 3 pounds cooked Black Beans
- 1 tbsp. lemon juice
- 2 teaspoons Garlic
- 2 teaspoons Salt
- 1/2 tsp. Black Pepper, Ground
- 2 teaspoons Chili Powder
- 1 tbsp. tapioca flour
- 2 tbsp. Water

Instructions

Place coconut oil, onion, carrot, and bell pepper in a stock pot. Cook the veggies until tender. Bring broth to a boil. Add cooked beans, broth and the remaining ingredients (except tapioca flour and 2 tbsp. water) to the vegetables. Bring that mixture to a simmer and cook approximately 15 minutes. Puree 1 quart of the soup in a blender and put back into the pot. Combine the tapioca flour and 2 tbsp. water in a separate bowl. Add the tapioca flour mixture to the bean soup and bring to a boil for 1 minute.

Ajoblanco con uvas - Almond and garlic soup-*White Gazpacho*

Serves 4-6

Ingredients - Allergies: SF, GF, DF, EF, V

- 1 cup flax seeds meal
- 200 g almonds, blanched and skinned
- 3 cloves garlic
- 150 ml extra virgin olive oil or avocado oil
- 5 tbsp. lemon juice
- 2 tsp salt
- 1 liter water
- 150 g grapes, seeded

Instructions

Put flax meal with the almonds and garlic in the blender. Blend to a smooth paste. Add a little water if necessary. Add the oil in a slow stream with the motor running. Add the lemon juice and salt too. Pour the mixture into a pitcher and add the remaining water. Add salt or lemon juice to taste. Chill the soup. Stir before serving and garnish with grapes.

Squash soup

Serves 4-6

Ingredients - Allergies: SF, GF, DF, EF, V, NF

- 1 Squash
- 1 carrot, chopped
- 1 onion (diced)
- 3/4 – 1 cup coconut milk
- 1/4 – 1/2 cup water
- olive oil or avocado oil
- Salt
- Pepper
- Cinnamon
- Turmeric

Instructions

Cut the squash and spoon out the seeds. Cut it into large pieces and place on a baking sheet. Sprinkle with salt, olive oil, and pepper and bake at 375 degrees F until soft (approx. 1 hour). Let cool.

In the meantime, sauté the onions in olive oil (put it in a soup pot). Add the carrots. Add 3/4 cup coconut milk and 1/4 cup water after few minutes and let simmer. Scoop the squash out of its skin. Add it to the soup pot. Stir to combine the ingredients and let simmer a few minutes. Add more milk or water if needed. Season to taste with the salt, pepper and spices. Blend until smooth and creamy.

Sprinkle it with toasted pumpkin seeds.

Egg-Drop Soup

Serves 4-6

Ingredients - Allergies: SF, GF, DF, NF

- 1 1/2 quarts vegetable broth
- 2 tbsps. Tapioca flour, mixed in 1/4 cup cold water
- 2 eggs, slightly beaten with a fork
- 2 scallions, chopped, including green ends

Instructions

Bring broth to a boil. Slowly pour in the tapioca flour mixture while stirring the broth. The broth should thicken. Reduce heat and let it simmer. Mix in the eggs very slowly while stirring. As soon as the last drop of egg is in, turn off the heat. Serve with chopped scallions on top.

Creamy Tomato Basil Soup

Serves 6

Ingredients - Allergies: SF, GF, DF, EF, V, NF

- 4 tomatoes - peeled, seeded and diced
- 4 cups tomato juice*
- 14 leaves fresh basil
- 1 cup coconut cream
- salt to taste
- ground black pepper to taste

Instructions

Combine tomatoes and tomato juice in stock pot. Simmer 30 minutes. Puree mixture with basil leaves in a processor. Put back in a stock pot and add coconut cream. Add salt and pepper to taste.

Minestrone

Serves 8-10

Ingredients - Allergies: SF, GF, DF, EF, NF

- 3 tbsp. coconut oil
- 3 cloves garlic, chopped
- 2 onions, chopped
- 2 cups chopped celery
- 5 carrots, sliced
- 2 cups vegetable broth
- 2 cups water
- 4 cups tomato sauce
- 1/2 oz. red wine (optional)
- 1 cup cooked kidney beans
- 2 cups green beans
- 2 cups baby spinach, rinsed
- 3 zucchinis, quartered and sliced
- 1 tbsp. chopped oregano
- 2 tbsp. chopped basil
- salt and pepper to taste
- 1 tbsp. olive oil or cumin oil

Instructions

Heat coconut oil over medium heat in a stock pot, and sauté garlic for few minutes. Add onion and sauté for few more minutes. Add celery and carrots and sauté for 2 minutes.
Add vegetable broth, tomato sauce and water and bring to boil, stirring frequently. Add red wine at this point. Reduce heat to low and add kidney beans, zucchini, green beans, spinach leaves,

oregano, basil, salt and pepper. Simmer for 30 to 40 minutes.

Stews, Chilies and Curries

Stuffed Peppers with beans

Serves 2

Ingredients - Allergies: SF, GF, DF, EF, V, NF

2 large red or green bell peppers
1 cup stewed tomatoes
1/3 cup brown rice
2 tbsp. hot water
2 green onions
8 ounces cooked black beans
1/4 tsp. crushed red pepper flakes
Instructions

Discard seeds and membrane from peppers. Place cut-side down and cover. Bake at 375F for 15 minutes.
While the peppers are cooking, cook tomatoes, rice and water for 15 minutes. In the meantime, thinly slice green onions.
Stir beans, green onions, and pepper flakes into tomato mixture. Cook for 10 minutes more. Drain peppers. Turn cut-side up. Spoon beans mixture evenly into peppers and bake in the oven for 5-10 minutes.

Vegetarian Chili

Serves 4-6

Ingredients - Allergies: SF, GF, DF, EF, V, NF

1 tbsp. coconut oil
1 cup chopped onions
3/4 cup chopped carrots
3 cloves garlic, minced
1 cup chopped green bell pepper
1 cup chopped red bell pepper
3/4 cup chopped celery
1 tbsp. chili powder
1-1/2 cups chopped mushrooms
3 cups chopped tomatoes
2 cups cooked kidney beans
1 tbsp. ground cumin
1-1/2 teaspoons oregano
1-1/2 teaspoons crushed basil leaves

Instructions

Heat coconut oil in a large saucepan and add onions, carrots and garlic; sauté until tender. Stir in green pepper, red pepper, celery and chili powder.
Cook, stirring often, until vegetables are tender, about 6 minutes. To the vegetables add mushrooms; cook 4 minutes. Stir in tomatoes, kidney beans, corn, cumin, oregano and basil. Bring to a boil. Reduce heat to medium. Cover and simmer for 20 minutes, stirring occasionally.

30-Minute Squash Cauliflower and Green Peppers Coconut Curry

Serves: 6

Ingredients - Allergies: SF, GF, DF, EF, V, NF

- Curry Paste
- 3 cups peeled, chopped squash
- 2 cups thick coconut milk
- 3 tbsp. coconut oil
- 2 tbsp. raw honey
- 2 pounds tomatoes
- 1 and 1/4 cup brown rice, uncooked
- 1 cup chopped Cauliflower
- 1 cup chopped Green Peppers
- Cilantro for topping

Instructions

Cook brown rice. Set aside.

Make Curry Paste. Pour the coconut milk into the skillet and mix the curry and raw honey into the coconut milk. Add the cauliflower, squash, and green peppers. Cover and simmer until squash is tender. Remove from heat and let stand for 10 minutes. The sauce will thicken.

Serve the curry over brown rice. Add chopped cilantro before serving.

Easy Lentil Dhal

Serves: 6

Ingredients - Allergies: SF, GF, DF, EF, V, NF

- 2 1/2 cups lentils
- 5-6 cups of water
- Curry Paste *
- 1/2 cup coconut milk
- 1/3 cup water
- 1/2 teaspoons salt + 1/4 tsp. black pepper
- lime juice
- Cilantro and spring onions for garnish

Instructions

Bring the water to a boil in a large pot. Add lentils and cook uncovered for 10 minutes, stirring frequently. Remove from heat. Stir in remaining ingredients. Season with salt and herbs for garnish.

Chickpea Curry

Serves 4

Ingredients - Allergies: SF, GF, DF, EF, V, NF

• Curry Paste

• 4 cups cooked chickpeas
• 1 cup chopped cilantro

Instructions

Make Curry Paste. Mix in chickpeas and their liquid. Continue to cook. Stir until all ingredients are blended. Remove from heat. Stir in cilantro just before serving, reserving 1 tbsp. for garnish.

Ratatouille

Serves 4-6

Ingredients - Allergies: SF, GF, DF, EF, V, NF

- 2 large eggplants
- 3 medium zucchinis
- 2 medium onions
- 2 red or green peppers
- 4 large tomatoes
- 2 cloves garlic, crushed
- 4 tbsp. coconut oil
- 1 tbsp. fresh basil
- Salt and freshly milled black pepper

Instructions

Cut eggplant and zucchini into 1 inch slices. Then cut each slice in half. Salt them and leave them for one hour. The salt will draw out the bitterness.

Chop peppers and onions. Skin the tomatoes by boiling them for few minutes. Then quarter them, take out the seeds and chop the flesh. Fry garlic and the onions in the coconut oil in a saucepan for a 10 minutes. Add the peppers. Dry the eggplant and zucchini and add them to the saucepan. Add the basil, salt and pepper. Stir and simmer for half an hour.

Add the tomato flesh, check the seasoning and cook for an additional 15 minutes with the lid off.

Frijoles Charros

Serves 4-6

Ingredients - Allergies: SF, GF, DF, EF, NF

- 1 pound dry pinto beans

- 5 cloves garlic, chopped

- 1 tsp. salt

- 1 onion, chopped & 2 fresh tomatoes, diced

- few sliced sliced jalapeno peppers

- 1/3 cup chopped cilantro

Instructions

Place pinto beans in a slow cooker. Cover with water. Mix in garlic and salt. Cover, and cook 1 hour on High.

Place oil and onion in the skillet. Cook until tender. Mix in jalapenos and tomatoes. Cook until heated through. Transfer to the slow cooker and stir into the beans. Continue cooking for 4 hours on Low. Mix in cilantro about half an hour before the end of the cook time.

Brown Rice Dishes

Serves 4-6

Asparagus Mint Lemon Risotto

Serves 6-8

Ingredients - Allergies: SF, GF, DF, EF, NF

For the risotto base

- 1 liter vegetable broth
- 2 tbsp. olive oil or cumin oil
- 1 large onion, peeled and finely chopped
- 4-5 sticks celery, trimmed and finely chopped
- 600 g brown rice
- 250 ml dry white wine

For the risotto

- 2 bunches asparagus, woody ends removed and discarded
- 700 ml vegetable broth
- 50 g coconut oil
- 1 bunch fresh mint, leaves picked and finely chopped
- zest and juice of 2 lemons
- sea salt
- ground black pepper
- extra virgin olive oil or avocado oil

Instructions

Chop asparagus discs, keeping the tips whole. Bring the broth to a simmer in a saucepan. Put the olive oil in a separate pan, add the celery and the onion and cook until soft. Add the rice and wine and turn up the heat and keep stirring.
Add the broth to the rice a ladle at a time, stir well and wait until it has been absorbed. When it's all absorbed, put to one side.
Put a saucepan on high heat and pour in half the broth, followed by all risotto base and the asparagus. Simmer until almost all the broth has been absorbed. Add the rest of the broth in batches until the rice and asparagus are cooked. Turn off the heat, add olive oil, mint, lemon zest and all the juice. Check the seasoning and add salt and pepper if needed.

Garbanzo Stir Fry

Serves 2

Ingredients - Allergies: SF, GF, DF, EF, V, NF

- 2 tbsp. coconut oil
- 1 tbsp. oregano
- 1 tbsp. chopped basil
- 1 clove garlic, crushed
- ground black pepper to taste
- 2 cups cooked garbanzo beans

- 1 large zucchini, halved and sliced
- 1/2 cup sliced mushrooms
- 1 tbsp. chopped cilantro
- 1 tomato, chopped

Heat oil in a skillet over medium heat. Stir in oregano, basil, garlic and pepper. Add the garbanzo beans and zucchini, stirring well to coat with oil and herbs. Cook for 10 minutes, stirring occasionally. Stir in mushrooms and cilantro; cook 10 minutes, stirring occasionally. Place the chopped tomato on top of the mixture to steam. Cover and cook 5 minutes more.

Mushrooms Casserole

Instructions – serves 4 - Allergies: SF, GF, NF

- 3 pounds sliced mushrooms (shiitake preferably)
- 1 pound sliced leeks
- Salt and freshly ground black pepper
- 1 tbsp. chopped parsley
- 2 beaten eggs
- 1 cup of low-fat Greek yogurt
- 1/2 cup of shredded cheddar cheese, low-fat

Instructions

Heat oven to 375 degrees F. Mix beaten eggs and low-fat yogurt in a separate dish. In a casserole, place 1 layer of mushrooms and leeks and season with salt, pepper, and parsley. Cover with 1/2 of a cup of eggs/yogurt mixture. Repeat process 2 more times and cover with shredded cheese. Bake until mushrooms is tender and crust is golden brown. Serve with Large Fiber Loaded salad with Italian Dressing.

Nutrition Facts

Serving Size 647 g

Amount Per Serving

Calories 325   Calories from Fat 55

% **Daily Value***

Total Fat 6.1g	**9%**
Saturated Fat 1.7g	**9%**
Trans Fat 0.0g	
Cholesterol 143mg	**48%**
Sodium 520mg	**22%**
Potassium 1426mg	**41%**
Total Carbohydrates 30.8g	**10%**
Dietary Fiber 5.5g	**22%**
Sugars 13.5g	
Protein 44.9g	

Vitamin A 41%   •   Vitamin C 43%

Calcium 23%   •   Iron 74%

Nutrition Grade A

* Based on a 2000 calorie diet

Pizza

Caulilower Pizza

Serves 4

Ingredients - Allergies: SF, GF, EF, NF

- 2 cups cauliflower

- 1 cup low-fat cheddar, shredded

- 1 tbsp. minced onion & few basil leaves

- 1 tsp garlic minced

Instructions

Preheat oven to 425 degrees Fahrenheit.

Grate half of the large cauliflower (2 cups approximately) and steam it for 15 minutes. Squeeze the excess water out and let cool. Mix in 2 eggs, one cup low-fat mozzarella, and salt and pepper. Pat into a 10-inch round on the prepared cookie sheet. Brush with oil and bake until golden. Add the topping as above.

Side dishes

Green Superfoods Rice

Serves: 8

Ingredients - Allergies: SF, GF, DF, EF, V, NF

- 1 cup spinach or any other leafy greens
- 1 cup leeks
- 1/2 cup or more cilantro leaves or parsley
- 1 jalapeno or serrano pepper
- 2 cloves garlic
- 1/4 cup coconut oil
- 1 cup brown rice
- 1 cup quinoa
- 3 tbsp flax seeds meal
- 3 cups water
- 1/2 tsp. salt (more to taste)

Instructions

Pulse the spinach, leeks, cilantro, pepper, and garlic in a food processor. Do it until they become very finely chopped.

Heat the oil in a pot over high heat. Add the rice and quinoa and stir continuously for 5-8 minutes, until the rice is starting to turn light golden brown. Add the water, salt. Cover and boil for 5 minutes. Stir, and lower the heat to simmer for another 10 minutes. Stir in the green paste from the step 1 and cook until the rice is fluffy. Serve with additional salt, cilantro leaves, and lime if desired.

Roasted curried cauliflower

Serves 10

Ingredients - Allergies: SF, GF, DF, EF, NF

- 12 cups cauliflower florets
- 1 chopped large onion
- 1 tsp. coriander seeds
- 1 tsp. cumin seeds
- 3/4 cup <u>olive</u> oil or <u>avocado</u> oil
- 1/2 cup lemon juice
- 3 1/2 teaspoons curry paste
- 1 tbsp. hot paprika
- 1 3/4 teaspoons salt
- 1/4 cup chopped cilantro

Instructions

Heat oven to 450°F. Place cauliflower florets in large roasting pan. Add onions to cauliflower. Dry toast coriander and cumin seeds in a skillet over medium heat until slightly browned, about 5 minutes. Crush in mortar with pestle. Place seeds in bowl. Whisk in oil, lemon juice, curry paste, paprika, and salt. Pour dressing over vegetables and toss to coat. Spread vegetables in single layer and sprinkle with pepper.

Roast vegetables until tender, stirring occasionally, about 35 minutes.

Sprinkle cilantro and serve warm.

Roasted cauliflower with Tahini sauce

Serves 6

Ingredients - Allergies: SF, GF, DF, EF, V, NF

- 1/4 cup extra-virgin <u>olive</u> oil or <u>avocado</u> oil
- 4 tsp. ground cumin
- 2 heads cauliflower, cored and cut into 1 1/2" florets
- Salt and ground black pepper
- 1/2 cup tahini
- 3 cloves garlic, smashed and minced into a paste
- Juice of 1 lemon

Instructions

Roast cauliflower like in the previous recipe.
Meanwhile, combine tahini, lemon juice, garlic, and 1/2 cup water in a bowl and season with salt. Serve cauliflower hot or at room temperature with tahini sauce.

Baked Sweet Potatoes

Serves 2

Ingredients - Allergies: SF, GF, DF, EF, V, NF

- 2 medium sweet potatoes

Instructions

Heat oven to 425 degrees F. Quarter sweet potatoes and place them in a casserole with a lid. Bake until tender when pierced with a fork (40 minutes approx.).

Asparagus with mushrooms and hazelnuts

Serves 4

Ingredients - Allergies: SF, GF, DF, EF, V

- 2 tbsp. lemon juice
- 1/4 tsp sea salt
- Ground black pepper, to taste
- 1 pound fresh asparagus, ends trimmed
- 2 tbsp. coconut oil
- 6 cups mushrooms
- 1/2 cup green onions, sliced
- 2 tbsp. hazelnuts, toasted and finely chopped

Instructions

Add the lemon juice, 1 tbsp. of the oil, salt, and pepper in a small bowl. Boil water in a pan and add the asparagus. Boil for few minutes. Heat the remaining 1 tbsp. oil in a pan on high heat. Add mushrooms and cook them until they are soft. Add green onions and sauté 1 more minute. Add the asparagus, and cook another 3 minutes. Remove from the heat and slowly add in the lemon juice mixture. Add the toasted hazelnuts over the top.

Chard and Cashew Sauté

Serves 2

Ingredients - Allergies: SF, GF, DF, EF, V, NF

- 1 bunch Swiss chard
- 1/2 cup cashews
- 1 tbsp. coconut oil
- Sea salt (optional)
- Ground black pepper

Instructions

Wash Swiss chard and remove tough stems. Heat a skillet over medium heat, and add oil when hot. Chop Swiss chard into thin strips. Add Swiss chard to the hot skillet, along with cashews. Sauté only 1 minute. Season with sea salt and ground black pepper to taste and serve warm.

Cauliflower rice side dish

Serves 2

Ingredients - Allergies: SF, GF, DF, EF, V, NF

- 1 head cauliflower
- 2 Tbs coconut oil
- Sea salt, garlic, ginger or ground black pepper (optional seasonings)

Instructions

Place the cauliflower into a food processor and pulse it until a grainy rice-like consistency. Season with sea salt and ground black pepper. Meanwhile, heat a large sauté pan over high heat. Add coconut oil when hot. Sauté cauliflower in a pan with oil and any additional seasonings if desired.

Crockpot

Sweets

Sweet Superfoods pie crust

Ingredients - Allergies: SF, GF, DF

- 11/3 cups blanched almond flour
- 1/3 cup tapioca flour
- 1/2 tsp. sea salt
- 1 large egg
- 1/4 cup coconut oil
- 2 tbsp. coconut sugar or raw honey
- 1 tsp of ground vanilla bean

Instructions

Place almond flour, tapioca flour, sea salt, vanilla, egg and coconut sugar (if you use coconut sugar) in the bowl of a food processor. Process 2-3 times to combine. Add oil and raw honey (if you use raw honey) and pulse with several one-second pulses and then let the food processor run until the mixture comes together. Pour dough onto a sheet of plastic wrap. Wrap and then press the dough into a 9-inch disk. Refrigerate for 30 minutes.

Remove plastic wrap. Press dough onto the bottom and up the sides of a 9-inch buttered pie dish. Crimp a little bit the edges of crust. Cool in the refrigerator for 20 minutes. Put the oven rack to middle position and preheat oven to 375F. Put in the oven and bake until golden brown.

Apple Pie

Serving Size: Serves 8

Ingredients - Allergies: SF, GF, DF

For the Crust: See previous recipe

For the Apple Filling:

- 2 tbsp. coconut oil
- 9 sour apples, peeled, cored and cut into 1/4-inch thick slices
- 1/4 cup coconut sugar or raw honey
- 1/2 tsp. cinnamon
- 1/8 tsp. sea salt
- 1/2 cup coconut milk

For the Topping:

- 1 cup ground nuts and seeds

Instructions

Filling: Melt coconut oil in a large pot over medium heat. Add apples, coconut sugar or raw honey, cinnamon and sea salt. Increase heat to medium-high and cook, stirring occasionally, until apples release their moisture and sugar is melted. Pour coconut milk or cream over apples and continue to cook until apples are soft and liquid has thickened, about 5 minutes, stirring occasionally.

Pour the filling into the crust and then top with topping. Place a pie shield over the edges of the crust to avoid burning. Bake until topping is just turning golden brown. Cool and serve.

Superfoods Dark Chocolate

Instructions - Allergies: SF, GF, DF, EF, V, NF

Mix 1/4 cup of coconut oil with 1/4 to 1/2 cup of cocoa powder (unsweetened, ideally organic and unprocessed) and some raw honey to taste. You really should experiment with cocoa and honey amount. Maybe start with equal amount of coconut oil, cocoa and honey, mix it and then increase amount of cocoa to your taste. Form balls or put in the ice cube tray. Put it in the fridge and 1 hour later you'll have great homemade Superfoods chocolate!

Fruits dipped in Superfoods chocolate

Ingredients - Allergies: SF, GF, DF, EF, V

- 2 apples or 2 bananas or a bowl of strawberries or any fruit that can be dipped in melted chocolate
- 1/2 cup of melted superfoods chocolate (see earlier recipe)
- 2 tbsp. chopped nuts (almond, walnut, Brazil nuts) or seeds (hemp, chia, sesame, flax seeds meal)

Instructions

Cut apple in wedges or cut banana in quarters. Melt the chocolate and chop the nuts. Dip fruit in chocolate, sprinkle with nuts or seeds and lay on tray. Transfer the tray to the fridge so the chocolate can harden; serve. If you don't want chocolate, cover fruits with almond or sunflower butter and sprinkle with chia or hemp seeds and cut it into chunks and serve.

Superfoods No-Bake Cookies

Ingredients - Allergies: SF, GF, DF, EF, V

- 1/2 cup coconut milk

- 1/2 cup cocoa powder

- 1/2 cup coconut oil

- 1/2 cup raw honey

- 2 cups finely shredded coconut

- 1 cup large flake coconut

- 2 tsp of ground vanilla bean

- 1/2 cup chopped almonds or chia seeds (optional)

- 1/2 cup almond butter (optional)

Instructions

Combine the coconut milk, coconut oil and cacao powder in a saucepan. Cook the mixture over medium heat, stirring until it comes to a boil and then boil for 1 minute. Remove the mixture from the heat and stir in the shredded coconut, large flake coconut, raw honey and the vanilla. Add additional ingredients if you want. Spoon the mixture to a parchment lined baking sheet to cool.

Raw Brownies

Ingredients - Allergies: SF, GF, DF, EF, V

- 1 1/2 cups walnuts
- 1 cup pitted dates
- 1 1/2 tsp. ground vanilla bean
- 1/3 cup unsweetened cocoa powder
- 1/3 cup almond butter

Instructions

Add walnuts and salt to a food processor or blender. Mix until finely ground.

Add the vanilla, dates, and cocoa powder to the blender. Mix well and optionally add a couple drops of water at a time to make the mixture stick together.

Transfer the mixture into a pan and top with almond butter.

Superfoods Ice cream

Allergies: SF, GF, DF, EF, V, NF

Freeze a banana cut into chunks and process it in blender once frozen and add half a tsp. of cinnamon or 1 tsp. of cocoa or both and eat it as ice-cream.

Other option would be to add one spoon of <u>almond</u> butter and mix it with mashed banana, it's also a delicious ice cream.

Apple Spice Cookies

Ingredients - Allergies: SF, GF, DF, EF, V

- 1 cup unsweetened almond butter
- 1/2 cup raw honey
- 1 egg & 1/2 tsp salt
- 1 apple, diced
- 1 tsp cinnamon
- 1/4 tsp ground cloves
- 1/8 tsp nutmeg
- 1 tsp fresh ginger, grated

Instructions

Heat oven to 350 degrees F. Combine almond butter, egg, raw honey and salt in a bowl. Add apple, spices, and ginger and stir. Spoon batter onto a baking sheet 1 inches apart. Bake until set. Remove cookies and allow to cool on a cooling rack.

Superfoods Macaroons

Ingredients - Allergies: SF, GF, DF, NF

- 3 egg whites

- 1/2 cup coconut sugar

- 1/4 tsp. salt

- 1 cup unsweetened flaked coconut

- 1/2 cup soft dried apricots, coarsely chopped (3 ounces)

Heat the oven to 325 degrees. Whisk together egg whites, sugar, and salt in a bowl until frothy. Add apricots and coconut and mix to combine.

Shape mixture into mounds with hands and place one inch apart on baking sheet.

Bake until lightly golden, 35 to 40 minutes. Rotate sheet halfway through. You can cover them with Superfoods Dark Chocolate.

Superfoods Stuffed Apples

Allergies: SF, GF, DF, EF, V

Core 10 apples, fill them with Superfoods No Bake Balls mix and bake them in the oven for 25-30 minutes.

Whipped Coconut cream

Ingredients - Allergies: SF, GF, DF, EF, V, NF

- 4 cups of any fresh berries
- 2 lemons
- 1 can full fat coconut milk (14 oz.), refrigerated overnight
- 1 tsp of ground <u>vanilla</u> bean
- 2 Tbsp. raw <u>honey</u>
- Dash of cardamom, nutmeg and clove (optional)

Instructions

Separate coconut cream from the milk by putting it overnight in the fridge. Don't shake it before opening.

Open the can of coconut milk and scrape out the cream into a bowl. Use the saved milk for smoothies or other recipes.

Add cardamom, raw honey and vanilla. Whip the cream with a hand mixer until fluffy. Put in the fridge.

Wash berries and place in serving bowls or glasses. Squeeze the lemon over the berries. Place a big scoop of cream on top of the berries and serve.

Granola Mix

Ingredients - Allergies: SF, GF, DF, EF, V

- 10 Cup Rolled Oats
- 1/2 Pound Shredded Coconut
- 2 Cup Raw Sunflower Seeds
- 1 Cup Sesame Seeds or chia seeds
- 3 Cup Chopped Nuts
- 1-1/2 Cup -Water
- 1-1/2 Cup coconut oil
- 1 Cup raw honey
- 1-1/2 Tsp. Salt
- 2 Tsp. Cinnamon
- 1 tbsp. of ground vanilla bean

- Dried cranberries

Instructions

Turn the oven on and heat oven to 300F. Combine oats, coconut, sunflower seeds, sesame seed, cranberries and nuts (can include almonds, pecans, walnuts, or a combination of all of them). Blend well.
Combine water, oil, raw honey, salt, cinnamon and vanilla in a large pan. Heat until raw honey is dissolved, but don't boil.
Pour the honey over the dry ingredients and stir well. Spread onto cookie sheets. Bake 25 to 30 minutes, and stir occasionally. Let it cool. Store in a cool dry place.

Pumpkin pie

Ingredients - Allergies: SF, GF, DF, NF

- 11/2 cup homemade pumpkin puree
- 3 eggs
- 1/2 cup coconut milk
- 1/2 cup raw honey
- 1 tbsp. ground cinnamon
- 1 tsp. nutmeg
- ⅛ tsp. sea salt
- 1 Superfoods Sweet Pie Crust, unbaked

Instructions

In a food processor combine pumpkin puree, and eggs. Pulse in cinnamon, nutmeg, coconut milk, raw honey, and salt. Pour filling into Superfoods Sweet Pie Crust and bake at 350° for 45 minutes. Allow the pie to cool and then refrigerate for 2 hours.

178 | P a g e

Blueberry Cream Pie

Ingredients - Allergies: SF, GF, DF, EF, V, NF

- Sweet Superfoods pie crust

  Filling:

- 2 Teaspoons plant-based gelatin, dissolved in 2 Tbsp. hot water

- 1/3 cup lemon juice

- 1/3 cup raw honey

- 1 can coconut milk, chilled

- 4 cups blueberries for serving

Instructions

Mix the gelatin and water together. Stir to dissolve and add the lemon juice. Whip coconut milk and raw honey with electric mixer about 15 minutes. Add the gelatin to the whipped cream. Pour the filling into the crust. Filling will set up in the refrigerator.

Chill for at 4 hours until set, and serve with lots of berries.

Upside down Apple Cake

Ingredients - Allergies: SF, GF, DF

Bottom Fruit Layer:

- 2 tbsp. coconut oil, melted
- 1 apple, sliced, or 1/4 cup blueberries, plums, banana etc.
- 2 tbsp. walnut chunks
- 2 tbsp. coconut sugar
- 1 tsp ground cinnamon.

Top Cake Layer:

- 2 eggs, beaten.
- 1/3 cup raw honey
- 1/4 cup unsweetened coconut milk, or unsweetened almond milk.
- 1 tsp ground vanilla bean
- 1 tsp lemon juice.
- 1 banana, mashed, or 1/4 cup blueberries
- 1/3 cup coconut flour

Instructions

Heat the oven (350 F), and grease a 9 inch cake pan.

Place 2 tbsps. coconut oil into cake pan, and put pan into preheating oven for a couple minutes to melt oil. Make sure oil is evenly distributed all over the bottom of the pan.

Sprinkle 2 tbsps. coconut sugar all over the oil.

Sprinkle 1 tsp cinnamon on top of sweetened layer.

Layer apple slices or blueberries on top of sweetened layer. Add optional walnut pieces to fruit layer. Set aside.

Combine all the "top cake layer" ingredients in a large mixing bowl except for the coconut flour. Mix and add the coconut flour and mix well.

Spoon batter on top of fruit layer and spread evenly.

Bake until center is set.

Remove from oven and let cool.

Slide a butter knife between cake and edge of pan to loosen cake. Turn cake pan upside down onto a large plate or serving platter. Cake should fall onto plate. If not, use spatula to take the cake out.

Raw Vegan Reese's Cups

"Peanut" Butter Filling

- 1/2 cup sunflower seeds butter
- 1/2 cup almond butter
- 1 Tbsp. raw honey
- 2 Tbsp. melted coconut oil

Superfoods Chocolate Part:

- 1/2 cup cacao powder
- 2 Tbsp. raw honey
- 1/3 cup coconut oil (melted)

Instructions

Mix the "Peanut" butter filling ingredients. Put a spoonful of the mixture into each muffin cup.

Refrigerate. Mix Superfoods chocolate ingredients. Put a spoonful of the Superfoods chocolate mixture over the "peanut" butter mixture. Freeze!

Raw Vegan Coffee Cashew Cream Cake

Coffee Cashew Cream

- 2 cups raw cashews
- 1 tsp. of ground vanilla bean
- 3 tablespoons melted coconut oil
- 1/4 cup raw honey
- 1/3 cup very strong coffee or triple espresso shot

Crust

See recipe for Raw Walnuts Pie Crust

Instructions

Blend all ingredients for the cream, pour it onto the crust and refrigerate. Garnish with coffee beans.

Raw Vegan Chocolate Cashew Truffles

Ingredients

- 1 cup ground cashews
- 1 tsp. of ground vanilla bean
- 1/2 cup coconut oil
- 1/4 cup raw honey
- 2 tbsp. flax seeds meal
- 2 tbsp. hemp hearts
- 2 tbsp. cacao powder

Instructions

Mix all ingredients and make truffles. Sprinkle coconut flakes on top.

Raw Vegan Double Almond Raw Chocolate Tart

Ingredients

- 1½ cups raw almonds
- ¼ cup coconut oil, melted
- 1 tablespoon raw honey or royal jelly
- 8 ounces dark chocolate, chopped
- 1 cup coconut milk
- 1/2 cup unsweetened shredded coconut

Instructions

Crust

Ground almonds and add melted coconut oil, raw honey and combine. Using a spatula, spread this mixture into the tart or pie pan.

Filling

Put chopped chocolate in a bowl, heat coconut milk and pour over chocolate and whisk together. Pour filling into tart shell. Refrigerate. Toast almond slivers chips and sprinkle over tart.

Raw Vegan Bounty Bars

"Peanut" Butter Filling

- 2 cups desiccated coconut
- 3 Tbsp. coconut oil - melted
- 1 cup coconut cream - full fat
- 4 Tbsp. of raw honey
- 1 Tsp. ground vanilla bean
- pinch of sea salt

Superfoods Chocolate Part:

- 1/2 cup cacao powder
- 2 Tbsp. raw honey
- 1/3 cup coconut oil (melted)

Instructions

Mix coconut oil, coconut cream, honey, vanilla and salt. Pour over desiccated coconut and mix well. Mold coconut mixture into balls, small bars similar to bounty and freeze. Or pour whole mixture into a tray, freeze and cut into small bars.

Make Superfoods Chocolate mixture, warm it up and dip frozen coconut into chocolate and put on a tray and freeze again.

Raw Vegan Tartlets with Coconut Cream

Crust:

See recipe for Raw Walnuts Pie Crust. Make tartlets.

Pudding:

- 1 avocado

- 2 tablespoons coconut oil

- 2 tablespoons raw honey

- 2 tablespoons cacao powder

- 1 teaspoon ground vanilla bean

- Pinch of salt

- 1/4 cup Almond milk, as needed

Coconut cream:

See recipe for "Whipped Coconut Cream". Add 1/2 tsp. cinnamon and whip again.

To make the pudding: blend all the ingredients in the food processor until smooth and thick. Spread evenly into tartlet crusts. Optionally, put some goji berries on top of the pudding layer.

Make the coconut cream, spread it on top of the pudding layer, and put back in the fridge overnight. Serve with one blueberry on top of each tartlet.

Raw Vegan "Peanut" Butter Truffles

Ingredients

- 5 tbsp. sunflower seed butter
- 1 tbsp. coconut oil
- 1 tbsp. raw honey
- 1 teaspoons ground vanilla bean
- 3/4 cup almond flour
- 1 tbsp. flax seeds meal
- pinch of salt
- 1 tbsp. cacao butter
- hemp hearts (optional)
- 1/4 cup Superfoods Chocolate

Instructions

Add sunflower seed butter, coconut oil, raw honey, vanilla, almond flour, flaxseed meal and salt to a large bowl.

Mix until all ingredients are incorporated.

Roll the dough into 1-inch balls, place them on parchment paper and refrigerate for half an hour (yield about 14 truffles)

Dip each truffle in the melted Superfoods Chocolate, one at the time, and place them back on the pan with parchment paper or coat them in cocoa powder or coconut flakes.

Raw Vegan Chocolate Pie

Crust

- 2 cups almonds, soaked overnight and drained
- 1 cup pitted dates, soaked overnight and drained
- 1 cup chopped dried apricots
- 1 1/2 tsp. ground vanilla bean
- 2 tsp. chia seeds
- 1 banana

Filling

- 4 Tbsp. raw cacao powder
- 3 Tbsp. raw honey
- 2 ripe avocados
- 2 Tbsp. organic coconut oil
- 2 Tbsp. almond milk (if needed, check for consistency first)

Instructions

Add almonds and banana to a food processor or blender. Mix until it forms a thick ball. Add the vanilla, dates, and apricot chunks to the blender. Mix well and optionally add a couple drops of water at a time to make the mixture stick together.

Spread in a 10 inch dis.

Mix filling ingredients in a blender and add almond milk if necessary. Add filling to the crust and refrigerate.

Raw Vegan Chocolate Walnut Truffles

Ingredients

- 1 cup ground walnuts
- 1 tsp. cinnamon
- 1/2 cup coconut oil
- 1/4 cup raw honey
- 2 tbsp. chia seeds
- 2 tbsp. cacao powder

Instructions

Mix all ingredients and make truffles. Coat with cinnamon, coconut flakes or chopped almonds.

Your Free Gift

As a way of saying thanks for your purchase, I'm offering you my FREE eBook that is exclusive to my book and blog readers.

Superfoods Cookbook Book Two has over 70 Superfoods recipes and complements Superfoods Cookbook Book One and it contains Superfoods Salads, Superfoods Smoothies and Superfoods Deserts with ultra-healthy non-refined ingredients. All ingredients are 100% Superfoods.

It also contains Superfoods Reference book which is organized by Superfoods (more than 60 of them, with the list of their benefits), Superfoods spices, all vitamins, minerals and antioxidants. Superfoods Reference Book lists Superfoods that can help with 12 diseases and 9 types of cancer.

http://www.SuperfoodsToday.com/FREE

Other Books from this Author

Superfoods Today Diet is a Kindle Superfoods Diet <u>book</u> that gives you 4 week Superfoods Diet meal plan as well as 2 weeks maintenance meal plan and recipes for weight loss success. It is an extension of Detox book and it's written for people who want to switch to Superfoods lifestyle.

Superfoods Today Body Care is a Kindle <u>book</u> with over 50 Natural Recipes for beautiful skin and hair. It has body scrubs, facial masks and hair care recipes made with the best Superfoods like avocado honey, coconut, olive oil, oatmeal, yogurt, banana and Superfoods herbs like lavender, rosemary, mint, sage, hibiscus, rose.

Superfoods Today Cookbook is a Kindle book that contains over 160 Superfoods recipes created with 100% Superfoods ingredients. Most of the meals can be prepared in under 30 minutes and some are really quick ones that can be done in 10 minutes only. Each recipe combines Superfoods ingredients that deliver astonishing amounts of antioxidants, essential fatty acids (like omega-3), minerals, vitamins, and more.

Superfoods Today Smoothies is a Kindle Superfoods Smoothies book with over 70+ 100% Superfoods smoothies. Featured are Red, Purple, Green and Yellow Smoothies

Low Carb Recipes for Diabetics is a Kindle Superfoods <u>book</u> with Low Carb Recipes for Diabetics.

Diabetes Recipes is a Kindle Superfoods <u>book</u> with Superfoods Diabetes Recipes suitable for Diabetes Type-2.

Diabetic Cookbook for One is a Kindle Superfoods <u>book</u> with Diabetes Recipes for One suitable for Diabetes Type-2

Diabetic Meal Plans is a Kindle <u>book</u> with Superfoods Diabetes Meal Plans suitable for Diabetes Type-2

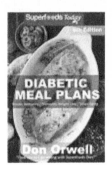

One Pot Cookbook is a Kindle Superfoods book with Superfoods One Pot Recipes.

Low Carb Dump Meals is a Kindle book with Low Carb Dump Meals Superfoods Recipes.

Superfoods Today Salads is a Kindle <u>book</u> that contains over 60 Superfoods Salads recipes created with 100% Superfoods ingredients. Most of the salads can be prepared in 10 minutes and most are measured for two. Each recipe combines Superfoods ingredients that deliver astonishing amounts of antioxidants, essential fatty acids (like omega-3), minerals, vitamins, and more.

Superfoods Today Kettlebells is a Kindle Kettlebells beginner's <u>book</u> aimed at 30+ office workers who want to improve their health and build stronger body without fat.

Superfoods Today Red Smoothies is a Kindle Superfoods Smoothies book with more than 40 Red Smoothies.

Superfoods Today 14 Days Detox is a Kindle Superfoods Detox book that gives you 2 week Superfoods Detox meal plan and recipes for Detox success.

Superfoods Today Yellow Smoothies is a Kindle Superfoods Smoothies book with more than 40 Yellow Smoothies.

Superfoods Today Green Smoothies is a Kindle Superfoods Smoothies book with more than 35 Green Smoothies.

Superfoods Today Purple Smoothies is a Kindle Superfoods Smoothies book with more than 40 Purple Smoothies.

Superfoods Cooking For Two is a Kindle book that contains over 150 Superfoods recipes for two created with 100% Superfoods ingredients.

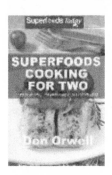

Nighttime Eater is a Kindle book that deals with Nighttime Eating Syndrome (NES). Don Orwell is a life-long Nighttime Eater that has lost his weight with Superfoods and engineered a solution around Nighttime Eating problem. Don still eats at night☺. Don't fight your nature, you can continue to eat at night, be binge free and maintain low weight.

Superfoods Today Smart Carbs 20 Days Detox is a Kindle Superfoods book that will teach you how to detox your body and start losing weight with Smart Carbs. The book has over 470+ pages with over 160+ 100% Superfoods recipes.

Superfoods Today Vegetarian Salads is a Kindle book that contains over 40 Superfoods Vegetarian Salads recipes created with 100% Superfoods ingredients. Most of the salads can be prepared in 10 minutes and most are measured for two.

Superfoods Today Vegan Salads is a Kindle book that contains over 30 Superfoods Vegan Salads recipes created with 100% Superfoods ingredients. Most of the salads can be prepared in 10 minutes and most are measured for two.

Superfoods Today Soups & Stews is a Kindle book that contains over 70 Superfoods Soups and Stews recipes created with 100% Superfoods ingredients.

Superfoods Desserts is a Kindle Superfoods Desserts book with more than 60 Superfoods Recipes.

Smoothies for Diabetics is a Kindle <u>book</u> that contains over 70 Superfoods Smoothies adjusted for diabetics.

50 Shades of Superfoods for Two is a Kindle <u>book</u> that contains over 150 Superfoods recipes for two created with 100% Superfoods ingredients.

50 Shades of Smoothies is a Kindle <u>book</u> that contains over 70 Superfoods Smoothies.

50 Shades of Superfoods Salads is a Kindle <u>book</u> that contains over 60 Superfoods Salads recipes created with 100% Superfoods ingredients. Most of the salads can be prepared in 10 minutes and most are measured for two. Each recipe combines Superfoods ingredients that deliver astonishing amounts of antioxidants, essential fatty acids (like omega-3), minerals, vitamins, and more.

Superfoods Vegan Desserts is a Kindle Vegan Dessert <u>book</u> with 100% Vegan Superfoods Recipes.

Desserts for Two is a Kindle Superfoods Desserts <u>book</u> with more than 40 Superfoods Desserts Recipes for two.

Superfoods Paleo Cookbook is a Kindle Paleo <u>book</u> with more than 150 100% Superfoods Paleo Recipes.

Superfoods Breakfasts is a Kindle Superfoods <u>book</u> with more than 40 100% Superfoods Breakfasts Recipes.

Superfoods Dump Dinners is a Kindle Superfoods <u>book</u> with Superfoods Dump Dinners Recipes.

Healthy Desserts is a Kindle Desserts <u>book</u> with more than 50 100% Superfoods Healthy Desserts Recipes.

Superfoods Salads in a Jar is a Kindle Salads in a Jar <u>book</u> with more than 35 100% Superfoods Salads Recipes.

Smoothies for Kids is a Kindle Smoothies <u>book</u> with more than 80 100% Superfoods Smoothies for Kids Recipes.

Vegan Cookbook for Beginners is a Kindle Vegan <u>book</u> with more than 75 100% Superfoods Vegan Recipes.

Vegetarian Cooking for Beginners is a Kindle Vegetarian <u>book</u> with more than 150 100% Superfoods Paleo Recipes.

Foods for Diabetics is a Kindle book with more than 170 100% Superfoods Diabetics Recipes.

Healthy Kids Cookbook is a Kindle book with Superfoods Kids friendly Recipes.

Superfoods Beans Recipes is a Kindle <u>book</u> with Superfoods Beans Recipes.

Diabetic Slow Cooker Recipes is a Kindle <u>book</u> with Superfoods Slow Cooker Diabetic Recipes.

Ketogenic Crockpot Recipes is a Kindle <u>book</u> with Superfoods Ketogenic Crockpot Recipes.

Stir Fry Cooking is a Kindle <u>book</u> with Stir Fry Superfoods Recipes.

Sirt Food Diet Cookbook is a Kindle <u>book</u> with Superfoods Sirt Food Recipes.

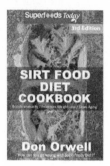

Made in United States
North Haven, CT
01 July 2022

20796027R00136